THE BIBLICAL BLUEPRINT FOR CORPORATE SUCCESS

TIMELESS WISDOM FOR EFFECTIVE COMMUNICATION

PRADEEP PRAVARTIK KASAB

BlueRose ONE
Stories Matter
NewDelhi • London

BLUEROSE PUBLISHERS
India | U.K.

BlueRose ONE
Stories Matter
NewDelhi • London

For permissions requests or inquiries regarding this publication, please contact:

BLUEROSE PUBLISHERS
www.BlueRoseONE.com
info@bluerosepublishers.com
+91 8882 898 898
+4407342408967

ISBN: 978-93-5989-768-4

Cover design: Rishav Rai
Typesetting: Rohit

First Edition: April 2024

The book, "The Biblical Blueprint for Corporate Success - Timeless Wisdom for Effective Communication," Is for educational and inspiring purposes only. The content draws from biblical stories and themes to illuminate corporate communication.

It is important to note that this book does not condemn, encourage, or hurt any religious group. Interpretations are subjective and susceptible to interpretation. The author accepts religious diversity and promotes courteous and inclusive conversation.

Readers should keep an open mind because biblical narratives might be interpreted differently.

Remember that the interpretations and applications of biblical stories may vary among individuals. The author intends to inspire and educate, without any intention to challenge or undermine any religious beliefs.

We hope that readers of all faiths and backgrounds will find value in the insights shared within these pages.

By reading this book, you acknowledge and accept the intent of the author and Publisher.

•••

Foreword:

By Rev. Nana Dar

...

It is my privilege and honour to write the forward for this book "The Biblical Blueprint for Corporate Success" - Timeless Wisdom for Effective Communication.

The pages of this book reveal a glimpse to the reader about the biblical importance to every Christian person who is working in the corporate world. A world is filled with modern ideas, thought patterns and a life of compromise at every stage to keep our job no matter what.

This book has revealed the necessity of learning success by following the Biblical blueprint for corporate success.

The Bible Says in 2 Timothy 3:15-17 "That the man of God may be perfect, thoroughly furnished unto all good works." This scripture is used to preach in theological preaching. But this book helps us to understand and be equipped as a common person who believes in God and who is working in the corporate world, how to understand the word of God which also takes care of the person to guide him to be successful in his life in the corporate world.

The author has very well explained different areas of our life and character to be used from the biblical learnings in our day-to-day life, such as the life of Joseph, Naomi and Ruth, Daniel, Job, the Story of the Good Samaritan from the New Testament, Moses' Leadership, The Life of David, and Paul's instructions to Timothy.

I have been blessed by this book. The Author has written to take care to help all those who are working in the corporate world to be living witnesses as Jesus has said in **Matthew 5:14-16** " Let your life **SO SHINE** before men (In Your Corporate World) that they may see **YOUR GOOD WORKS AND GLORIFY YOUR HEAVENLY FATHER."**

May God bless everyone who will read and follow these directions from the Word of God.

Book Summary:

•••

Success in today's fast-paced business environment hinges on the ability to communicate effectively. It moulds connections, encourages teamwork, and lays the groundwork for career growth. This book sets out on a quest to discover the timeless principles of effective communication, drawing inspiration from an ancient source of wisdom—the Bible.

Reading "The Biblical Blueprint for Corporate Success" is like taking a guided tour of the Bible's ageless wisdom. It dives into important ideas, explaining them thoroughly and providing examples from the business world to show how they apply.

Several characters in the Bible exemplify the talent of efficient communication: Joseph, who listened attentively, Naomi and Ruth, who were devoted and gentle, and Daniel, who was always genuine and honest. The timeless and universal wisdom found in the Bible's stories is not limited to any one religion or culture; rather, it may be applied to every aspect of life and work.

Corporate workers, executives, and everyone else who wants to foster a compassionate and ethical workplace should read this book. Its advice is designed to help people succeed in the business world. It's a guide to surmounting obstacles, building deeper connections, and succeeding in a cutthroat work environment.

An enthralling manual, "The Biblical Blueprint for Corporate Success" brings together timeless teachings with modern business practices, providing a new angle on how to connect with others and communicate effectively. Anyone looking to further their careers and foster a more cooperative and fruitful work environment will find this book to be an invaluable resource.

The Bible doesn't provide a specific list of life skills for effective communication, but it does offer guidance on principles that can help improve communication. Some of these principles include:

- **Listening:** Proverbs 18:13 says, "To answer before listening—that is folly and shame." Actively listening to others is a key component of effective communication.
- **Kindness and Gentleness:** Ephesians 4:32 advises, "Be kind and compassionate to one another." Treating others with kindness and gentleness can foster better communication.
- **Honesty and Truthfulness:** Ephesians 4:25 encourages, "Therefore each of you must put off falsehood and speak truthfully." Honesty is crucial for effective communication.
- **Patience:** Proverbs 15:1 teaches, "A gentle answer turns away wrath, but a harsh word stirs up anger." Being patient in conversations can prevent conflicts and promote effective communication.
- **Empathy:** Philippians 2:4 advises, "Let each of you look not only to his own interests but also to the interests of others." Understanding others' perspectives and feelings is vital for communication.

- **Clarity:** 1 Corinthians 14:9 emphasizes the importance of clear speech: "So it is with you. Unless you speak intelligible words with your tongue, how will anyone know what you are saying?" Clarity in communication is key.
- **Self-Control:** Proverbs 29:11 states, "A fool gives full vent to his anger, but a wise man keeps himself under control." Maintaining self-control during conversations can lead to more effective communication.
- **Building Lasting Relationships:** Ephesians 4:29 emphasizes the importance of wholesome and edifying communication. Open and honest communication is crucial for building trust and understanding in relationships.

While the Bible doesn't provide a comprehensive list of communication skills, it offers valuable guidance on how to interact with others constructively and compassionately.

Introduction:

...

The ability to communicate effectively and interact with others is essential to achieving success in the business world, which is constantly changing because of the constant evolution of the terrain. Not only is the capacity to connect, comprehend, and work together with other people essential to professional success, but it is also essential to the development of harmonious and productive working conditions when it comes to the workplace.

In this book, we go on a journey through the ancient wisdom of the Bible, discovering insights into the art of communication that are essential to our understanding of the subject. The Bible, which is a source of eternal truths and lessons, offers a rich tapestry of stories and themes that can serve as a guide for us as we navigate the complexity of modern corporate life.

The purpose of each chapter in this book is to delve into a particular ability or concept that is derived from the Bible. It provides explanations, examples, and practical counsel for how these skills and principles might be applied in the business world. The more we learn about the lives and experiences of biblical figures, the more we discover teachings that are universal and transcend both period and culture.

The active listening of Joseph, the self-control of David, the empathy of the Good Samaritan, and the honesty of Daniel are just a few of the examples that we find in the Bible that provide a wealth of guidance that can enable individuals to flourish in the business world. These concepts are not limited to any particular faith but rather are universal in nature. They provide a road map for efficient communication and the development of relationships that will last lifetimes.

This book is intended to give you the tools and insights you need to achieve your goals, whether you are an employee looking to grow both personally and professionally, a leader who wants to motivate and direct your team, or someone who wants to establish a corporate culture that is founded on ethics and compassion.

We invite you to join us as we investigate how the wisdom of the Bible might be applied to the modern business environment. It is through our collective efforts that we will uncover the enduring power of these concepts, which not only affect how we communicate but also how we achieve success in the business environment.

Contents

...

Chapter 1:
Listening Skills

•••

The story of Joseph is found in the Book of Genesis in the Old Testament, primarily in Genesis chapters 37 to 50. While the direct theme of "listening skills" may not be explicit, Joseph's story does contain instances where listening, understanding, and interpreting messages play significant roles. Here are key verses related to Joseph's experiences:

- Genesis 37:5-11: Joseph has dreams that he shares with his brothers, and they interpret these dreams as symbols of Joseph's future authority. However, their initial lack of understanding and jealousy sets the stage for future events.

- Genesis 37:12-36: Joseph's brothers plot against him due to their jealousy. Reuben, one of the brothers, intervenes to save Joseph from harm, demonstrating a mix of misunderstanding and some level of consideration.

- Genesis 39:6b-23: In Potiphar's house, Joseph demonstrates listening and understanding by resisting the advances of Potiphar's wife, choosing to honour God's commandments.

- Genesis 41:1-57: Joseph interprets Pharaoh's dreams, showcasing his ability to listen to divine revelation and provide wise counsel. This skill leads to his appointment as a high-ranking official in Egypt.

- Genesis 45:1-15: Joseph reveals his true identity to his brothers, demonstrating a deep understanding of their changed hearts. He emphasizes God's plan in the events that transpired.
- Genesis 50:15-21: After their father's death, Joseph's brothers fear his retaliation. Joseph reassures them, demonstrating forgiveness and a listening heart to their concerns.

While the story of Joseph is rich in various themes, these verses highlight instances where Joseph's listening skills, whether in dreams or in interpreting the intentions of others, played a crucial role in the unfolding narrative.

The Story of Joseph:

Joseph is a fascinating individual in the Bible who is noted for his ability to interpret dreams. He is the son of Jacob and Rachel. Joseph's tale is a great illustration of the effectiveness of active listening when it comes to the context of a business setting. During his trip, Joseph goes from being sold into slavery by his brothers to rising through the ranks to become the second-in-command in Egypt.

Joseph's natural ability to interpret dreams stems from his ability to pay close attention to what others have to say. He paid close attention to the dreams of two other convicts while he was incarcerated. These inmates were the head baker and the chief cupbearer. In addition to hearing the words, he endeavoured to comprehend the more profound meanings that were concealed inside the dreams. As a result of his attentive listening, he was able to correctly interpret the dreams, which ultimately drew the notice of Pharaoh.

The narrative of Joseph demonstrates the significance of not just listening to what is being spoken but also empathising with the feelings, requirements, and points of view of the person who is speaking. When applied in a business setting, active listening may result in a deeper comprehension of one's coworkers and customers, which in turn can help to cultivate trust and offer up new prospects.

The emergence of Joseph in Egypt, which was driven by his ability to listen and interpret, demonstrates that good communication, particularly via listening, maybe a catalyst for both personal and professional development. The fact that he was able to decipher the meanings of dreams led to his employment as a trusted counsellor to the Pharaoh, a position that had a significant impact on the destiny of Egypt as well as the lives of its people.

We may improve our efficacy as communicators and leaders in the business world by adhering to the following concepts, which are taught to us by Joseph's narrative.

These principles include listening attentively and gaining a knowledge of the requirements and hopes of individuals who are in our immediate vicinity:

The skill of active listening is a component of listening skills:

There is a tendency to underestimate the importance of the capacity to actively listen in the fast-paced world of business communication. Active listening, on the other hand, is the foundation upon which successful communication is constructed. We are going to dig into the profound art of active listening in this chapter. We are going to investigate the relevance of active listening in the business world and provide some practical suggestions on how to develop and perfect this essential ability.

Listening attentively is the unseen cornerstone of effective communication:

Listening actively involves more than just hearing the words being spoken; it also involves understanding the speaker's point of view, feelings, and the message that lies beyond the surface. It is a dynamic process that requires you to interact with the person who is speaking, to ask questions, and to provide feedback that displays your real interest in the topic being discussed.

Reasons Why Active Listening Is Important in the Business World:

One cannot exaggerate the necessity of active listening in the business sector, which is characterised by a fast-paced and sometimes chaotic environment. It helps to cultivate understanding, trust, and collaboration, all of which are essential in a business environment of any kind.

It is important to demonstrate to your coworkers and customers that their viewpoints and ideas are taken into consideration when you actively listen to them. The mere act of acknowledging someone's efforts may serve as a potent incentive for more collaboration and improved interpersonal connections inside the workplace. Listening attentively to clients or consumers enables one to have a more profound understanding of their requirements and to be in a better position to offer solutions that are geared towards addressing their issues.

Active listening has the potential to transform the dynamics of a team completely. This fosters an inclusive culture in which the thoughts and contributions of all individuals are respected. There is a correlation between employees who feel heard and increased levels of engagement and commitment to their work, which in turn leads to increased levels of job satisfaction and productivity.

Steps to Take to Improve Your Active Listening Skills:

1. Pay Attention to Getting a Feel for the Perspective of the Speaker

Concentrating your attention on the person who is speaking is the first step in active listening. There are a lot of things that might divert your attention in the business environment, such as ringing cell phones and impending deadlines. On the other hand, to actively listen, you need to put these distractions aside and give the person who is speaking your undivided attention. Focus your gaze on the person in front of you, lean in close, and communicate via your body language that you are there.

Beyond the speaker's physical presence, you should completely submerge yourself in their point of view. Make an effort to imagine the situation from their point of view. Through the use of this empathic technique, you will be able to comprehend not only the words that are uttered but also the feelings and the reasons that lie behind them.

2. Inquire Questions That Will Clarify

Even the most skilled active listeners are prone to making mistakes in their interpretation of signals. This is where the skill of asking questions that are intended to explain something comes into play. When something is not obvious or seems to contradict itself, it is important to seek an explanation.

It is crucial that you properly phrase your asking queries. Instead of questioning, you should ask questions that show that you are interested in fully comprehending the situation. An example of a question that you may ask is, "Could you elaborate on that point?" or "Am I understanding correctly that...?"

Two skills are required to master the art of asking questions that explain something. To begin, it enhances the likelihood that you have correctly comprehended the message conveyed by the speaker. In the second place, it demonstrates to the person who is speaking that you care about their point of view, which promotes communication that is open and honest.

Practices of Active Listening: Obstacles to Overcome and Possible Solutions

Even while active listening is extremely important, it is not without its difficulties. Time restrictions, various duties, and technology distractions are common factors that make it difficult to engage in active listening in the business sector.

You have several options available to you to triumph over these obstacles:

- Listening should be placed first: It is important to schedule time in meetings or one-on-one conversations, particularly for active listening.
- Turn off any electronic devices and clean your workplace of any potential disruptions. This will help you eliminate as many distractions as possible.
- Mindfulness is the practice of training your mind to be present and attentive to the conversation that is now taking place.

The ability to engage in attentive listening is a fundamental component of successful corporate communication. Not only does it encourage comprehension, trust, and teamwork, but it also gives you the ability to comprehend the underlying meaning that lies beneath the words that are said. This ability may be developed and improved upon by concentrating on the viewpoint of the speaker and by employing clarifying questions. This will allow you to realise the full potential of this talent in your professional life.

In the business world, it is possible to differentiate yourself as a communicator and a collaborator by mastering the skill of active listening. This is a talent that not only enhances your performance but also makes the working atmosphere more amicable and productive for everyone involved.

Dismantling Obstacles to Engaging in Active Listening:

When it comes to active listening, practising it in a business environment can be especially difficult owing to the many obstacles that are there. The following is a list of frequent challenges, along with some potential solutions to solve them:

- **Information Overload:** In this day and age of digital technology, we are constantly being inundated with information. To reduce the impact of this, you can set up information filters and give priority to the material that is pertinent to your interactions. To lessen the burden on your mind, concentrate on the most important particulars.
- **Preconceived conceptions:** When we engage in discussions, we frequently do so with judgements or preconceived assumptions in mind. Before engaging in a discussion, it is important to practise mindfulness by intentionally putting away any preconceived notions you

may have been harbouring. Maintain an open mind throughout every conversation.

- **Constraints on Time:** When one's calendar is packed, active listening may appear to be an unnecessary luxury. Investing time in active listening, on the other hand, might eventually save time by minimising the number of misunderstandings and disagreements that occur. Ensure that the quality of your interactions is prioritised above the number.
- **Distractions Caused by Emotions:** Emotional responses, such as tension, annoyance, or enthusiasm, can make it difficult to have an engaged listening experience. When you find yourself getting emotional, make sure to give yourself some time to recognise your feelings before coming back to the conversation with a clear head.

The Butterfly Effect of Active Listening:

Active listening has a butterfly effect on the situation when it comes to the business world, the influence of active listening frequently goes beyond the conversation that is currently taking place. If you take the time to carefully listen to your coworkers or customers, you will not only get a more profound comprehension, but you will also make it very evident that their viewpoints are significant. This helps to cultivate trust, which is essential for the development of long-lasting partnerships.

It is possible that engaging in active listening will result in creative problem-solving, improved decision-making, and increased levels of occupation satisfaction. The good work atmosphere that it contributes to, in which people feel valued and understood, is significantly enhanced.

One of the most important aspects of successful negotiations is active listening. You will be able to modify your approach to reach agreements that are advantageous to both parties if you have a solid understanding of the underlying issues and motives of the other side. It is possible that active listening may result in enhanced service, stronger connections, and eventually increased client retention when it is applied to interactions with customers.

The ability to effectively provide feedback is another benefit of active listening. Your ability to deliver feedback that is constructive, detailed, and well-received is directly proportional to the degree to which you fully comprehend the perspectives of your coworkers or members of the team.

Taking the Practice of Active Listening to Higher Levels

Take into consideration the following advanced approaches to fully succeed in active listening:

- **Paraphrasing:** Immediately following the conclusion of the speaker's presentation, you should rephrase their primary points to confirm that you have accurately received them. Not only does this make your comprehension clearer, but it also assures the speaker that you are fully involved in the conversation.
- **Cues beyond the verbal:** Body language, facial expressions, and tone of voice are examples of nonverbal clues that should be taken into consideration. It is possible that these indications can disclose feelings and

complexities that cannot be transmitted only via the use of words.

- **Reflective listening:** Involves reflecting the feelings displayed by the speaker to demonstrate empathy and comprehension. For instance, you may say something along the lines of, "I can see that you are frustrated about this issue."
- **Empathetic Listening:** Listening with empathy involves going beyond simply comprehending the words being spoken and instead empathising with the feelings that the speaker is experiencing. This more profound degree of connection has the potential to have a significant influence on the development of trust and rapport.

In conclusion, the ability to engage in active listening is a characteristic that is essential to effective communication in the business environment. To do so requires not just listening to the speaker but also comprehending their point of view and actively interacting with it. You may make the most of the possibilities of active listening by concentrating on the viewpoint of the person who is speaking and by asking questions that are intended to clarify. As a communicator and a collaborator, it is a talent that distinguishes you from others, and it also leads to a more peaceful and productive working environment.

Chapter 2:
Kindness and Gentleness

•••

The story of Ruth and Naomi is found in the Book of Ruth in the Bible. The primary verses that narrate this touching story are in the Book of Ruth, chapters 1 to 4. Here are the specific references:

- Ruth 1:1-22: This chapter introduces the characters and sets the stage for the events that follow. It includes Naomi's journey with her daughters-in-law, Orpah and Ruth.
- Ruth 2:1-23: This chapter tells of Ruth's gleaning in the fields of Boaz, a relative of Naomi, which becomes a significant part of their story.
- Ruth 3:1-18: In this chapter, Naomi instructs Ruth on a plan to seek Boaz's protection and, potentially, marriage.
- Ruth 4:1-22: The final chapter concludes the story, detailing the legal proceedings at the city gate where Boaz redeems Ruth and marries her, securing the family line.

The Book of Ruth is a beautiful narrative that highlights themes of loyalty, kindness, and God's providence in the lives of ordinary people.

The Story of Ruth and Naomi

Ruth and Naomi's story is a heartwarming narrative of the compassion and faithfulness that they displayed towards one another. Specifically, it demonstrates how these characteristics may play a crucial role in the modern business environment.

Ruth, a Moabite lady, married into Naomi's household and found herself in the position of a widow. Ruth decided to remain with Naomi, her mother-in-law who had recently lost her husband, rather than go back to her country as her sister-in-law Orpah did. The choice that was made was a remarkable demonstration of both kindness and dedication. It was a demonstration of Ruth's dedication to providing Naomi with assistance during her time of need.

Within the framework of a business setting, this narrative emphasises the significance of being kind and compassionate when it comes to establishing connections and working together as a group. Ruth's compassion for Naomi served as the basis for their friendship, which was built on that foundation. An example of how acts of kindness may build a pleasant and supportive environment is the fact that she is eager to assist others, despite the difficulties she is experiencing in her own life.

Not only does Ruth's narrative convey the importance of compassion, but it also demonstrates the need for adaptation and the capacity to accept new circumstances. Ruth accompanied Naomi on her journey back to Bethlehem, and because of her generosity and unwavering commitment, she earned the affection and respect of the town. The fact that she was able to show that gentleness and compassion can be applied across cultural and societal borders is a lesson that may be extremely useful in the context of varied business organisations.

Naomi was not only able to gain directly from Ruth's deeds, but they also contributed to Naomi's success. Her tale is a testament to the idea that compassion and loyalty may open doors to chances in both one's personal life and one's professional life. She finally married Boaz, a prominent man in their town, and her story is a living example of this concept.

A helpful and cooperative work atmosphere may be created via acts of compassion and tenderness, as seen by the narrative of Ruth and Naomi, which should be taught to employees of corporations. Individuals are encouraged to go above and beyond to assist their coworkers and customers, with the awareness that these characteristics may have a big influence on their careers as well as the general performance of the organisation. This is accomplished by adhering to the concepts that are following:

Understanding the Benefits of Kindness and Gentleness in the Workplace Relationships

In the harsh world of business, compassion and gentleness may appear to be weaknesses but they are strengths. On the other hand, these characteristics serve as the foundation around which durable and flourishing relationships are constructed. Explore how these qualities have a beneficial influence on the dynamics of the workplace.

- **Trust and Respect:** Treating others with kindness and compassion creates an atmosphere in which trust and respect may flourish. Colleagues who treat one another with compassion are more inclined to trust one another and show respect for one another, which contributes to the creation of a pleasant environment at work. When it comes to effective cooperation and collaboration, trust is very necessary.

- **Employee Well-Being:** When employees are treated with kindness in the office, they report feeling a stronger sense of well-being. This is because compassion is at the forefront of professional relationships. The feeling that one is respected and cared for by one's coworkers and managers is associated with increased levels of job satisfaction and decreased levels of stress.
- **Conflict Resolution:** Conflicts in the workplace are unavoidable; yet, how they are managed differs significantly from one situation to another. The use of kindness and gentleness could defuse difficult situations, making it simpler to locate areas of agreement and arrive at solutions that are satisfactory to all parties concerned.
- **Improvements in Communication:** Being kind inspires others to communicate openly and honestly. When workers can freely voice their opinions and concerns without fear of retaliation, it fosters an environment that is conducive to the free flow of ideas and increases the likelihood of innovation and creativity.

Determining How to Handle Challenging Conversations with Grace

In the business world, it is impossible to avoid having challenging talks. The ability to manage these talks with grace is necessary, whether it be to address performance difficulties, provide critical criticism, or settle disagreements. However, kindness and gentleness are not indicators of weakness; rather, they are strong instruments that may be utilised to approach difficult topics while still preserving respect and professionalism.

1. **Start with Empathy:** Empathic understanding is the cornerstone of a compassionate approach when dealing with challenging communications. Try to understand the situation from the viewpoint of the other person. Try to comprehend their emotions and worries, even if you do not share their viewpoint.

2. **Focus on Finding answers:** Instead of ruminating on the issue at hand, you should emphasize finding answers. Have the conversation with the mindset that it is a chance to work together to find a solution that is beneficial to all involved parties.

3. **Active listening**: The third step is to actively listen to the perspective of the other person. Demonstrate that you are enthusiastic about comprehending their point of view. In addition to validating their sentiments, this also contributes to the development of trust.

4. **Pay Attention to Your Language:** The words you select to use in a challenging conversation can have a major influence on the result of the conversation. Make use of language that is neutral and avoids conflict. Instead of using language that is accusatory or offensive, prioritise beneficial communication.

The Difficulties and Solutions Involved in Kindness and Gentleness

The use of compassion and gentleness in the business world is not without its difficulties. There is a possibility that certain persons would view these characteristics as flaws, or they may react with aggressiveness. But there are ways to get around these obstacles, including the following:

- Establishing a Culture of Compassion Leadership is an essential component in the process of establishing a culture that is characterised by gentleness and compassion. Organisations can encourage the general adoption of these attributes if they emphasise their development from the top down.

- Investing in training programmes that assist employees in developing their emotional intelligence, empathy, and communication skills is the second step in the training and development process. By doing so, they are more equipped to successfully handle challenging interactions.
- Personal Resilience: By cultivating personal resilience, individuals can improve their capacity to demonstrate compassion and gentleness towards others. This entails engaging in activities that cultivate self-awareness and self-regulation to keep one's calm under difficult circumstances.

To summarise, compassion and gentleness are not seen to be weaknesses in the business world; rather, they are considered to be vital advantages. They are the foundations upon which trust, respect, and the well-being of employees are built. These characteristics provide important skills for navigating challenging discussions with empathy, communication that is focused on finding solutions, active listening, and mindful language. Through the adoption of these virtues, individuals and organisations can cultivate robust relationships, find solutions to problems, and establish an atmosphere that is conducive to the growth of trust and collaboration.

Kindness and gentleness are not expenses; rather, they are investments.

Kindness and gentleness should not be regarded as expenditures of time or resources; rather, they should be regarded as investments that bring enormous returns. They provide a contribution to a culture in the workplace that encourages people to feel respected, safe, and driven to perform their best.

1. **The retention of talent:** When working in an atmosphere that is characterised by acts of compassion and gentleness, employees are more inclined to remain with the organisation. The high staff turnover rate can be expensive in terms of the costs associated with recruiting, training, and the loss of institutional expertise.

2. **Engagement of Employees:** Employees who are engaged in their jobs are more devoted to their work and their productivity. A workplace that is kind and kind creates settings that are conducive to the growth of engagement. It is more probable that employees will go the additional mile when they have the sense that they are supported.

3. **The Reputation of the Organisation:** The way an organisation handles its partners and workers is frequently reflected in the reputation of the organisation. When you have a good reputation, you may recruit top talent, clients, and partners, which gives you an advantage over your competitors.

4. **Creativity and innovation:** A culture that is kind and promotes an environment in which people are encouraged to openly interact and share their experiences and ideas. This typically results in increased innovation and creativity among employees because they feel secure taking risks that have been well-considered.

Facilitating the Development of Kindness and Gentleness in the Workplace

The following are some techniques that people and organisations might consider using to foster a culture of kindness and gentleness in the workplace:

- **Leading by Exemplary Behaviour:** Leaders need to lead with compassion and gentleness. Their actions serve as a model for each member of the organisation. When leaders demonstrate these characteristics, it inspires their staff to do the same via their actions.
- **Implement training programmes** that emphasize emotional intelligence, empathy, and effective communication is the second step in the training and development process. Employees can be equipped with the skills necessary to demonstrate kindness and gentleness in their interactions with others via the use of these programmes.
- **Reward and Recognition:** In the workplace, it is important to recognise and reward employees who demonstrate acts of compassion and gentleness. By doing so, the significance of these characteristics is reaffirmed, and others are inspired to demonstrate them themselves.
- **Encourage open and transparent communication** inside the organisation, since this is the fourth open communication recommendation. Among these measures is the establishment of channels via which employees may voice their concerns and offer feedback. Kindness and tenderness are more likely to grow in an environment like this one.

- **Procedures for Conflict Resolution:** Create procedures for conflict resolution that emphasize using a compassionate approach that is focused on finding solutions. To guarantee that even challenging interactions are handled with grace, it is important to train personnel in these standards.

Kindness and gentleness have a ripple effect on the world over.

The virtues of kindness and gentleness are not singular characteristics; rather, they have a domino effect that goes beyond the scope of individual encounters. There is the potential for these characteristics to have a beneficial impact not only on the culture of the organisation as a whole but also on the connections with customers and even on the community.

- A workplace that is characterised by kindness and gentleness frequently develops into a culture that is inclusive and collaborative. This is the first aspect of organisational culture. The level of investment that employees have in their jobs increases and disagreements are settled more amicably.

- Relationships with Customers: How workers interact with one another frequently extends to how they interact with customers. The cultivation of trust, loyalty, and positive word-of-mouth recommendations among customers is facilitated by encounters that are kind and kind.

- influence on the Community: Organisations that demonstrate kindness and gentleness frequently extend their good influence on the community using activities implemented as part of their corporate social responsibility programmes. Having a favourable public image and providing employees with a feeling of purpose are both brought about by this.

A Concluding Statement Regarding the Power of Kindness and Gentleness

The qualities of kindness and gentleness are not indicators of a lack of strength; rather, they are characteristics of powerful and successful leaders and organisations. In addition to making employees feel respected and protected, they also encourage them to perform to the best of their abilities. In the business world, these characteristics help to the retention of talent, the engagement of employees, the development of a positive organisational reputation, as well as for innovation and creativity.

Leadership by example, training and development, recognition, open communication, and standard operating procedures for dispute resolution are all necessary components in the process of cultivating kindness and gentleness in the workplace. Through the adoption of these characteristics, individuals and organisations have the potential to generate a positive ripple effect that goes beyond the confines of the workplace and into the wider society.

There is more to the business world than simply the bottom line; it is also about the people who are responsible for driving that line. Through the act of being kind and gentle, we invest in the health and prosperity of those individuals, and as a result, we ultimately find ourselves reaping the benefits of strong connections, loyalty, and a great reputation, all of which have the potential to differentiate an organisation in the very competitive business landscape of today.

Chapter 3:
Honesty and Truthfulness

...

The story of Daniel exemplifies honesty and truthfulness, particularly in the context of his commitment to God and his refusal to compromise his faith. The Book of Daniel, found in the Old Testament, contains several chapters that detail Daniel's life and experiences. The specific chapters that provide insights into Daniel's commitment to honesty and truthfulness include:

- Daniel 1:8-16: In this passage, Daniel, along with his companions, faces a test regarding their diet. Daniel chooses to maintain his commitment to God's laws, demonstrating his honesty and dedication to his principles.
- Daniel 2:1-23: Daniel, with God's help, interprets King Nebuchadnezzar's dream. Daniel's honesty is evident as he attributes his ability to God and not to his wisdom.
- Daniel 6:1-28: The famous story of Daniel in the lions' den highlights his commitment to truthfulness. Daniel's unwavering devotion to praying to God results in him being thrown into the lions' den, but God delivers him.

These passages from the Book of Daniel illustrate the character of Daniel, who, throughout his life, consistently demonstrated honesty, truthfulness, and faithfulness to God despite challenging circumstances.

The Story of Daniel

A dramatic instance of the value of honesty and sincerity in the business world may be found in the narrative of Daniel, which is found in the Bible.

The young Israelite Daniel was taken captive in Babylon. He was taken captive there. It was when he was assigned to a high-ranking post in King Nebuchadnezzar's court that his unflinching dedication to his ideals and religion was put to the test. When Daniel refused to compromise his views by ingesting food and drink that contradicted the dietary limitations he had established for himself according to his religious beliefs, his integrity was on full display.

The story of Daniel highlights the significance of retaining honesty and integrity in the face of pressure or ethical difficulties in the setting of the business world. It is a powerful example of the power of ethical communication because he decided to convey his worries while still being true to his ideals.

Daniel made a name for himself in the eyes of the king of Babylon throughout his whole career in Babylon due to his honesty, intelligence, and ability to interpret dreams. During a royal feast, Daniel was the only one who was able to comprehend the handwriting that was written on the wall. This is one of the most well-known legends that involves Daniel. One of the most valued advisors to the king is Daniel, who is distinguished for his honesty and sincerity.

The story of Daniel reminds us that in the business world when it comes to establishing trust, respect, and credibility, honesty and integrity are necessary building blocks. Employees and executives who place a priority on these principles can negotiate difficult situations while maintaining their integrity. It was not just Daniel's unflinching dedication to his ideals that brought him personal success, but it was also to the advantage of the entire kingdom.

In their working life, workers of corporations are encouraged to remain steadfast in their adherence to their ethical ideals and principles, even when confronted with challenging choices or circumstances, as demonstrated by Daniel's example. This serves as a reminder to them that by adhering to the rules that are outlined below, they may increase their chances of gaining recognition, respect, and prospects for advancement within their respective organisations.

When it comes to the intricate realm of corporate communication, the values of honesty and truthfulness serve as unmovable pillars that serve as the foundation for trust, credibility, and ethical behaviour. The importance of honesty in establishing trust is discussed in depth in this chapter, along with several methods that may be utilised to ensure that sincerity is maintained in business communication.

The Importance of Being Honest in Instilling Trust

For a business connection to be successful, trust is essential. This holds whether the relationship is with coworkers, clients, partners, or stakeholders. As the act of communicating information without engaging in dishonesty or deception, honesty is the foundation upon which trust is built. Let us investigate the significant role that honesty plays in the business world and how it helps the growth of trust in corporate relationships.

- Credibility is established when individuals and organisations constantly speak the truth and follow their commitments. This increases the credibility of the individuals and organisations. In addition to being the foundation of trust, credibility is also the foundation of relationships that are strong and long-lasting.

- Conduct Based on Ethical Principles Being honest is not just about avoiding telling lies; it is also about adhering to a set of ethical principles. Establishing a reputation for integrity and dependability in the workplace via ethical behaviour in business communication is essential.
- Acceptance of responsibility Accepting responsibility for one's actions and decisions is an essential component of accountable communication. Because it indicates a desire to repair mistakes and preserve openness, this readiness to be held accountable helps to develop trust.

When workers, clients, and stakeholders are sure that they are receiving true information, they are more likely to engage fully in their professional interactions. This is because they are more likely to feel that they are obtaining accurate information. Confidence is a driving force behind successful collaboration and accomplishment.

Methods for Protecting the Integrity of Corporate Communication Strategies

To keep the integrity of business communication intact, it is necessary to make a conscious and unyielding commitment to ethical principles. The following are some solutions that people and organisations may implement to guarantee that honesty is always at the forefront of their relationships with one another.

- Leadership has a vital part in defining the culture of a company, and one of the most important roles is to promote an honest culture. Honesty and integrity should be modelled by those in positions of authority, and organisations should work to cultivate a culture that appreciates and encourages these characteristics.

- Emphasize transparency: communication that is both open and transparent is essential to honesty. Regardless of whether the information is challenging or unsettling, organisations have a responsibility to offer their workers and other stakeholders information that is both clear and honest.
- It is important to encourage workers and stakeholders to disclose unethical behaviour or concerns about dishonesty. Mechanisms for whistleblowing should be developed so that employees and stakeholders may report these concerns. It is a demonstration of a dedication to truthfulness to encourage people to blow the whistle.

Establishing and enforcing ethical norms of behaviour inside the organisation is the fourth objective of the ethical code enforcement process. It is imperative that every employee is aware of these norms and is aware of the repercussions that come with breaching them.

The Obstacles and Solutions to the Problem of Keeping One's Truthfulness

Even though honesty is a key principle in business communication, it is susceptible to assault for several different reasons. Listed below are some of the most prevalent problems and possible solutions:

- Fear of repercussions: Employees may be afraid that if they acknowledge making errors or being honest about difficulties, they will be subjected to adverse repercussions. Organisations need to establish a culture that prioritises honesty above punishment to overcome this issue.
- In the pursuit of corporate goals, employees may be motivated to overstate their accomplishments or underreport problems. This is because of the pressure that they are under to achieve their targets. In response to this, organisations ought to recognise and promote ethical behaviour and place a higher priority on long-term trust than they do on short-term wealth.
- Constraints imposed by legal and regulatory authorities Legal and regulatory considerations may place restrictions on the information that may be communicated inside a company. Under these circumstances, organisations want to make certain that they comply with all of the legal obligations while simultaneously preserving openness to the greatest degree that is feasible.
- Ethical Conundrums The field of corporate communication can give birth to a few difficult ethical conundrums. To assist employees in navigating such predicaments in a manner that is consistent with ethical norms, organisations ought to give guidance and training.

When it comes to the business world, honesty and candour are not only moral ideals; rather, they are necessary assets. The establishment of trust, trustworthiness, and ethical behaviour are all significantly aided by their assistance. The promotion of an honest culture, the emphasis on openness, the encouragement of whistleblowing, and the enforcement of ethical rules are all necessary components to maintain truthfulness in corporate communication. By adopting these tactics, individuals and organisations can promote the principles of honesty and truthfulness, therefore creating an atmosphere in which trust is fostered and ethical behaviour is valued.

Costs of deceit in corporate communication that are not readily apparent.

When it comes to business communication, we have already covered the various advantages that come with being honest and truthful. However, it is as important to acknowledge the hidden costs that come with being dishonest and lying. Although these costs are sometimes invisible, they have the potential to have far-reaching implications for both individuals and organisations.

- Harm to Reputation: When dishonesty is exposed, it has the potential to do significant harm to the reputation of an individual or organisation. To regain someone's trust after it has been broken can be a challenging and time-consuming endeavour.
- Secondly, the erosion of trust occurs when deceit is used, and this occurs not just in the present encounter but also in subsequent interactions. People are likely to become more sceptical and cautious in their interactions if they have experienced a violation of confidence.
- Legal and Regulatory Consequences Since dishonesty in business communication can sometimes have legal and regulatory ramifications, it is important to be aware of these potential outcomes. If you violate legal requirements

or engage in unethical acts, you may be subject to fines, lawsuits, and other different types of legal penalties.

- Disengagement of Employees and Stakeholders: When employees and stakeholders have the impression that they are being dishonest, they may become disengaged or demoralised or both. diminished productivity, diminished cooperation, and lower happiness are all potential outcomes of this disengagement.

Deceit can result in the loss of commercial possibilities, relationships, and collaborations. This is the fifth and last point under consideration. An individual or organisation that is perceived by individuals to be dishonest is less likely to be engaged with by those individuals.

Continually Working Towards Honesty and Truthfulness: A Struggle That Never Ends

Sincerity and honesty are not attributes that remain unchanged over time; rather, they call for continuous commitment and attention. It is crucial to recognise that these traits are not accomplished once and for all but are part of a continual journey. If individuals and organisations are working towards maintaining sincerity in corporate communication, it is necessary to acknowledge that this is a journey.

- Individuals should make it a habit to periodically reflect on their communication practices and behaviour to ensure that they are by the values and ethical standards that they have set for themselves.
- Learning from Errors: Although it is possible to make errors, it is essential to gain knowledge from them and to

take steps to rectify the situation. Recognising mistakes and taking responsibility for them are two of the most important aspects of an honest technique.

- Encourage your coworkers, clients, and other stakeholders to offer feedback on your communication using the third step, which is receiving feedback. Constructive criticism might bring to light issues that need to be improved.
- Mentorship and Training: Participate in mentoring or training programmes that place an emphasis on ethical communication and offer help on how to navigate complicated ethical challenges.

Take Advantage of the Benefits That Come With Being Honest and Truthful

Authenticity and integrity are the foundations upon which trust is built in the realm of business communication. The establishment of credibility, ethical behaviour, and accountability are all significantly aided by their contributions. To preserve truthfulness, it is necessary to foster an environment that values honesty, emphasizes openness, and strictly enforces ethical rules.

Even though there are obstacles to overcome to retain truthfulness, organisations and people may overcome these obstacles by cultivating a culture that places a high value on honesty, rewarding ethical behaviour, and giving advice and training.

When one embraces honesty and candour, it is not only about sticking to moral ideals; it is also about reaping the benefits of trust, credibility, and ethical behaviour. This pertains to the establishment of a setting in which individuals and organisations are acknowledged and valued for their honesty and dedication to being genuine in all forms of business communication.

Chapter 4:
Patience

•••

The story of Job, found in the Book of Job in the Old Testament, is a testament to patience and endurance in the face of immense suffering. The specific chapters in the Book of Job that narrate Job's story and highlight his patience include:

- Job 1:1-22: This chapter introduces Job as a righteous man who undergoes severe trials. Despite losing his wealth, children, and health, Job does not sin against God.
- Job 2:1-13: Job faces additional afflictions, including physical suffering. Yet, he remains patient and does not curse God.
- Job 3:1-26: In this chapter, Job expresses his deep distress and wishes he had never been born. It marks the beginning of a series of dialogues between Job and his friends.
- Job 42:1-17: The concluding chapter of the book depicts the resolution of Job's story. After enduring much suffering and engaging in dialogues with his friends, Job's patience is rewarded as God restores his fortunes.

The Book of Job is a profound exploration of the human experience of suffering and the virtue of patience. Despite the challenges Job faces, his patience and unwavering faith in God ultimately lead to his restoration.

The story of Job:

In the face of misfortune, the narrative of Job in the Bible offers a powerful illustration of the effects that may be achieved with patience. Although Job's narrative does not take place in a conventional corporate environment, the lessons that can be learned from it on patience and perseverance are extremely significant for the business world.

A guy of tremendous wealth, health, and pleasure, Job was a man of vast riches. Nevertheless, he was confronted with a string of calamitous challenges, such as the loss of his assets, his health, and even the support of his people, including his friends and family. Job had great patience and steadfast confidence in God throughout the entirety of his journey through suffering.

Within the framework of the business world, the narrative of Job highlights the significance of maintaining patience in the face of adversity. It is common for both employees and executives to experience challenges and obstacles in the context of a company environment that is constantly shifting and frequently unanticipated. Individuals can keep their calm, remain focused, and effectively work through problems when they can exercise patience in the face of hardship.

The narrative of Job also demonstrates the importance of patience in the process of dispute resolution. Even when confronted with incorrect advice and criticism from his friends, he maintained his patience and showed a willingness to engage in conversation. It is through his narrative that we are reminded that patience in communication may lead to greater understanding and settlement of disagreements, whether they are in the form of conflicts in the workplace or discussions with clients and partners.

Job's perseverance and faith ultimately resulted in his restoration and even greater wealth, despite the terrible pain he endured. Because it demonstrates that perseverance and patience may ultimately lead to success and personal development, his tale motivates people working in larger corporations.

The narrative of Job serves as a source of inspiration for those working in the business sector, encouraging them to continue and endure in the face of obstacles and difficulties. It serves as a reminder to them that patience is a virtue that may lead to both personal and professional success, and it can also serve as a guiding concept for understanding how to navigate the intricacies of the corporate world by adhering to the principles that are listed below:

Patience is a virtue that helps resolve conflicts more effectively.

Patience may be a resource that is in short supply in the world of business settings, which is frequently frantic. On the other hand, it is a potent virtue that not only improves the ability to resolve conflicts, but also cultivates a culture that values understanding, collaboration, and personal development. The purpose of this chapter is to examine the relevance of patience in business settings, to investigate the transforming role that patience plays in the settlement of conflicts, and to provide strategies for fostering patience.

In the process of conflict resolution, the power of patience

Differences in individuals' perspectives, objectives, and interests are the root cause of conflict, which is an unavoidable aspect of the business world. Having patience is the best way to deal with the confusion and anxiety that can be brought on by disagreements. Let's investigate the significant part that patience plays in the process of dispute resolution.

- The ability to regulate one's emotions Patience permits individuals to exert control over their feelings during times of conflict. This provides time to ponder and reply sensibly rather than emotionally, allowing for a pause before reacting impulsively and allowing for the opportunity to do so.
- Patience is a trait that cultivates greater communication, which is the second benefit. It is more probable that individuals will listen attentively to the opinions of others when they are patient, which may lead to communication that is productive, empathic, and constructive.
- Disagreement When it comes to de-escalating confrontations, patience is one of the most important factors to consider. It has the potential to prevent disputes from developing into damaging confrontations, therefore protecting relationships and maintaining productivity.
- Discovering Common Ground If individuals are patient, they will be able to discover areas of common ground and look for solutions that are good for both parties. Not only does it foster a focus on common goals, but it also discourages the perpetuation of contentious deadlocks.

In the context of business environments, strategies for cultivating patience

The cultivation of patience may appear to be difficult in the fast-paced and high-pressure world of business; nonetheless, it is vital for the settlement of conflicts and personal development. Here are some strategies that may be utilised in the business world to cultivate patience.

1. **Mindfulness and Self-Awareness:** Individuals can recognise and control their impatience when they engage in the practice of mindfulness and self-awareness. Practising mindfulness entails paying attention to one's thoughts, feelings, and bodily sensations, which may be beneficial in terms of managing reactions.

2. **Empathy:** Having the ability to empathise with the experience of others might help one become more patient. One way for individuals to improve their ability to handle disputes is to make an effort to comprehend the feelings and motives of their coworkers and stakeholders.

3. **Listening Actively:** Patience and attentive listening are two qualities that go hand in hand. Demonstrating respect for people and reducing stress may be accomplished by attentively listening to them without interrupting them.

4. **Time Management:** Being able to efficiently manage time can help decrease stress and lack of patience but is not essential. When you want to prevent the hurry that frequently results in frustration, you should prioritise work and set reasonable deadlines.

Developing Patience: Obstacles to Overcome and Possible Solutions

In business environments, patience may be tested by several different variables, even though it has many advantages. Listed below are some of the most prevalent problems and possible solutions:

- **High-stress organisations:** The fast-paced and high-stress nature of business organisations can make patience difficult to maintain. Strategies for managing stress, such as practising mindfulness and engaging in relaxation activities, are among the solutions.
- **Immediate Deadlines:** Immediate deadlines have the potential to increase frustration. One way to ease this strain is to practise effective time management and to create expectations that are in line with reality.
- **Diversity and Differences:** Differences in personality and culture might increase the likelihood of misunderstandings and irritation with one another. To foster understanding and patience among members of a diverse team, training and activities designed to develop teams might be beneficial.
- **The sense of inefficiency:** Another factor that might contribute to impatience is the perception of inefficiency. Clearly defining roles and duties, as well as optimising procedures, are potential solutions to this problem.

When it comes to the business environment, patience is a transforming virtue that plays a significant role in improving communication, dispute resolution, and teamwork. Being mindful, having self-awareness, having empathy, actively listening, and effectively managing one's time are all necessary components. The advantages of a more peaceful work environment, improved relationships, and successful conflict resolution make the cultivation of patience a beneficial investment for both individuals and organisations alike. This is true even though developing patience can be difficult.

The Influence of Patience on a Butterfly Effect

In the process of cultivating and practising patience, a ripple effect is created that reaches well beyond the settlement of conflicts. The effects of this impact are not only beneficial to the environment of the corporation, but they also have repercussions in the personal and professional lives of individuals.

- Enhanced Capacity for Decision-Making: Possessing patience allows one to make better decisions. People are more likely to be patient when they take the time to absorb information, evaluate alternatives, and consider the potential implications of their actions. Taking this technique with careful consideration typically results in judgements that are more informed and more successful.
- Improved Employee Well-Being: A climate at work that is patient and understanding is beneficial to the well-being of employees. There is a correlation between employees experiencing reduced stress and frustration, which leads to increased job satisfaction and productivity, and when they feel appreciated and heard by their employer.
- A healthy Work Culture: An organisation that understands the need for patience cultivates a healthy

work culture. Collaboration, creativity, and the retention of employees are all fostered by this culture. As a result, it creates an atmosphere in which people can freely share their thoughts and concerns without the fear of being judged in a fast manner.

- Reputation and Relationships with Customers: Customers and business partners value patience when it comes to interactions in the business world. When individuals and organisations demonstrate patience, they can construct robust and long-lasting connections that encompass customers, business partners, and other stakeholders.

Developing Patience as a Skill That Will Last a Lifetime

Patience is not only a talent that may be utilised in certain circumstances; rather, it is a skill that can be utilised throughout one's whole life and has the potential to improve every facet of one's personal and professional life. It is an investment in one's personal development as well as the development of harmonious relationships.

- Commit to lifelong education: This is a quest that lasts a lifetime: cultivating patience. Individuals should be willing to engage in ongoing learning, self-reflection, and personal growth to improve their proficiency in this area.

- Ask for Feedback and Mentorship: The second step is to ask for feedback from your coworkers and bosses on areas in which you may improve your patience. The assistance and mentoring of persons who have much experience in the practice of patience may be quite beneficial.

- Commemorate Successes: Recognise and rejoice in the accomplishments, both personal and professional, that were achieved through the application of patience throughout difficult times. Individuals can be motivated to continue their journey of progress by receiving this positive reinforcement.
- Have reasonable expectations: Be conscious of the significance of establishing attainable expectations. It is possible to decrease impatience by gaining an understanding that not everything can be completed instantaneously and that certain solutions take time.

Concluding remarks: Having patience may have a transformative effect.

Patience is not a sign of inactivity in business settings; rather, it is a skill that may be used to navigate problems, improve communication, and create a pleasant working atmosphere. Emotional control, improved communication, the de-escalation of conflict, and the identification of areas of agreement are all made possible as a result of this.

To cultivate patience, one must have self-awareness, empathy, the ability to actively listen, and the ability to effectively manage time. The benefits of cultivating patience include a more pleasant work culture, improved decision-making, and greater employee well-being. Despite the difficulties involved in learning patience, it is an investment that is certainly worth making.

Patience has a ripple effect that reaches well beyond the settlement of conflicts; it has a favourable influence on decision-making, employee well-being, work culture, and client relationships. Patience is not a one-time accomplishment but rather a talent that is acquired during one's whole life and, when developed, has the potential to improve both the personal and professional facets of an individual's life. This provides a demonstration of the transforming potential of patience, not only in the business sector but also in other contexts.

Chapter 5: Empathy

...

The story of the Good Samaritan is a well-known parable of Jesus found in the Gospel of Luke in the New Testament. The specific Bible verses that narrate the story of the Good Samaritan and highlight the theme of empathy include:

- Luke 10:25-37: This passage begins with a lawyer testing Jesus by asking what he must do to inherit eternal life. In response, Jesus tells the parable of the Good Samaritan. The Samaritan's actions demonstrate compassion, empathy, and kindness toward a man who had been beaten and left for dead, contrasting with the indifference of others.

The story emphasizes the importance of showing mercy and empathy to those in need, irrespective of social or cultural differences. The Good Samaritan's actions serve as an example of selfless love and care for one's neighbour.

The story of the Good Samaritan:

The story of the Good Samaritan, which is included in the New Testament and was related by Jesus, is an example of compassion and empathy that has stood the test of time. One may learn a valuable lesson about the necessity of empathy in the business world from experiencing this.

The protagonist of this fable is a traveller who is assaulted, battered, and abandoned on the side of the road; he is presumed dead. Without giving any aid, a few people, including a priest and a Levite, walk past the injured guy without offering any assistance. As is customary, the Samaritan, who is generally regarded as an adversary of the Jewish people, is the one who stops to assist the injured traveller. It is not only that he repairs the man's wounds, but he also offers shelter and care, and he even pays for the costs that were expended.

The deeds of the Good Samaritan serve as a prime example of the significance of empathy and compassion in the workplace, particularly in the setting of the business world. Empathy is not confined to trying to comprehend the viewpoints of other people; rather, it encompasses taking significant steps to alleviate the pain of others or to provide for their needs.

The tale of the Good Samaritan highlights the need for empathy in both organisational leadership and collaborative efforts. As the Good Samaritan went out of his way to assist a stranger, leaders who can empathise with the people of their team can cultivate an environment that is characterised by trust, collaboration, and support. To maintain unity and harmony in a varied corporate environment, it is vital to demonstrate compassion and understanding towards coworkers who come from a variety of backgrounds.

The lesson that may be learned from this fable is that empathy is not limited by social or cultural borders. When it comes to the business sector, empathy opens the door for employees and executives to engage with customers, business partners, and members of their teams on a more personal level. Because of this, they can comprehend the specific difficulties and goals that others are pursuing, which ultimately results in communication and collaboration that is more effective and meaningful.

The parable of the Good Samaritan serves as a useful reminder that empathy is an essential attribute for professionals to possess to achieve success in the business environment. Because of this, employees of corporations are encouraged to demonstrate compassion, consideration, and a willingness to go the additional mile to assist their coworkers, customers, and communities. Not only does this strategy improve professional relationships, but it also helps to foster a culture in the workplace that is more sympathetic and welcoming to all employees.

There is a compassionate catalyst for team collaboration and leadership, and that catalyst is empathy.

Empathy is a transformative skill that not only fosters greater team cooperation but also plays a crucial role in successful leadership. In the dynamic world of business environments, empathy stands out as a transformational quality that is indispensable. Within the context of the business world, this chapter dives into the value of empathy, examining how it improves the level of collaboration among members of a team and how it empowers leadership via compassion.

How to Improve Team Collaboration Through the Development of Empathy

When it comes to the success of a company, team cooperation is the most important factor, and empathy is the connective tissue that holds members of the team together. The deep impact that empathy plays in developing cooperation and boosting collaboration is something that we should investigate.

1. Understanding and Appreciate: Empathy inspires members of a team to understand and appreciate one another's points of view, as well as to recognise the differences that exist between them. As a result, the working environment becomes more welcoming and pleasant after this.

2. Effective Communication: Empathy enhances communication by encouraging attentive listening, open discourse, and the capacity to articulate ideas in a way that is both clear and sympathetic. The free flow of ideas and thoughts is encouraged as a result of this.

3. Conflict Resolution: It is unavoidable that disagreements will surface within the dynamics of the team. The members of the team can manage these disputes with understanding and compassion when they have empathy, which ultimately leads to outcomes that are beneficial to all parties involved.

4. Increased Creativity: Teams that demonstrate empathy tend to be more imaginative and creative than other teams. When members of a team show appreciation for one another's experiences and points of view, it results in a proliferation of different ways of thinking and new points of view.

Empathy in Leadership: Leading with Compassion and Understanding

Effective leadership goes beyond only exercising power; it also requires inspiring and encouraging others to perform to the best of their abilities. Empathy is a fundamental component of compassionate leadership since it enables leaders to comprehend the requirements and goals of the members of their team. Let us investigate how empathy may alter leadership.

- Trust and Loyalty: Leaders who demonstrate empathy are rewarded with increased trust and loyalty from the members of their team. When workers get the impression that their manager is concerned about their health and happiness, they are more engaged and dedicated to their work.
- Empathetic leaders make the health and happiness of their team members a top priority: the well-being of their employees. They acknowledge the difficulties that employees encounter and assist them in achieving a healthy balance between their personal and professional lives.
- Conflict Resolution: Caring and compassionate leaders can negotiate disagreements with grace and understanding. They recognise that disagreements are an inevitable component of the dynamics of the workplace and view them as chances for personal development and professional advancement.
- Decision-Making That Is Everyone's Responsibility Empathetic leaders include all members of their team in the decision-making process. They actively seek out a variety of perspectives and promote cooperation, which frequently results in judgements that are more informed and more productive.

Developing Empathy: Obstacles to Overcome and Possible Solutions

Although empathy is a powerful attribute, it may be difficult to apply in the business world due to the nature of the setting. Listed below are some of the most prevalent problems and possible solutions:

- The fast-paced nature of business environments might make it difficult to have sufficient time for in-depth empathy because of the time constraints that are there. Among the potential solutions is the allocation of a specific time for regularly scheduled team check-ins and open communication.
- Secondly, misunderstandings and assumptions can be a barrier to empathy. Misunderstandings and preconceptions can block empathy. It is important for teams to avoid making assumptions about the intentions or feelings of their colleagues and to aggressively seek clarification if there is a misunderstanding.
- Resistance to Change: Some members of the team may be resistant to or sceptical about an empathic leadership style. The advantages of empathy should be communicated by leaders, and they should also show the success of empathy and create opportunities for members of the team to adapt.
- Personal Biases: Personal biases have the potential to influence empathy. Teams and leaders need to participate in diversity and inclusion training in order to help eliminate unconscious prejudices and foster empathy for all members of the team.

The compassionate catalyst that fosters greater team collaboration and inspires leadership with compassion is empathy. Empathy nourishes better team cooperation. It results in increased creativity, understanding, and respect among team members, as well as better communication, conflict resolution, and settlement of disagreements. When it comes to leadership, empathy helps to develop trust, provides a priority to the well-being of employees, settles disagreements, and supports inclusive decision-making.

The cultivation of empathy necessitates the development of abilities in active listening, open discussion, and conflict resolution. The benefits of enhanced cooperation, trust, employee well-being, and inclusive decision-making make empathy a worthy investment for both individuals and organisations alike, despite the problems that it presents.

The Ripple Effect of Empathy in Corporate Environments

There is no such thing as a lonely attribute; rather, empathy is a ripple effect that extends its influence throughout corporate contexts, affecting both individual and organisational components.

1. **Empathy**: This is a powerful tool for improving the cohesiveness of a team. It is more probable that members of a team would work together amicably and encourage one another when they have the sense that they are understood and respected.

2. **Employee Engagement:** Leaders who demonstrate empathy can encourage increased workforce participation. Employees are more motivated and engaged in their jobs when they have the perception that their bosses care about their well-being.

3. **Invention and Creativity:** Creativity and invention are fostered in a society that is characterised by empathy. Those teams that value the unique perspectives and experiences of their members are often more inventive, which results in the generation of novel ideas and approaches.

The presence of empathy in the workplace is one of the factors that lead to a great culture in the workplace. When empathy is fostered and practised inside an organisation, it can mould the culture of the organisation, which in turn helps to attract and keep talented individuals and creates an atmosphere in which individuals may flourish.

Learning to Empathise as a Skill That Lasts a Lifetime

Empathy is not a talent that can be learned once and then left to remain stagnant; rather, it is a skill that is gained during one's whole life and requires continuous growth and development.

- **Self-awareness:** The first step in developing empathy is to become self-aware. To have a deeper comprehension of their emotional responses, individuals should engage in introspection into their feelings, thoughts, and behaviours.
- **Active and sympathetic Listening:** Active and sympathetic listening is a fundamental component of empathy. To encourage folks to be completely present and involved in discussions, it is important to encourage them to concentrate on comprehending the viewpoint of the speaker rather than generating replies.
- **Empathy-Building Exercises**: An organisation may conduct empathy-building exercises and activities to foster empathy among its personnel. Some examples of these exercises include role-playing, group discussions, and training programmes that are centred on empathy.
- **Learning and criticism**: A crucial component of the development of empathy is the provision of chances for

learning and constructive criticism. Encourage individuals to seek feedback on their ability to empathise with others, as well as to engage in opportunities for ongoing learning and personal development.

To summarise, the transformative power of compassionate understanding

Not only is empathy a trait that makes one feel good, but it is also a transforming force that improves team cooperation, cultivates leadership with compassion, and has a significant influence on the culture of a company as well as its level of business success. Understanding, respect, effective communication, and inclusive decision-making are all outcomes that result from this practice within teams. In the realm of leadership, empathy fosters trust, places a priority on the well-being of employees, offers a resolution to problems, and inspires creativity.

Active listening, open communication, and the capacity to resolve disagreements with grace are all activities that contribute to the cultivation of empathy. Empathy is an investment that is beneficial for both individuals and organisations alike since, despite the difficulties, it results in greater cooperation, trust, employee engagement, creativity, and a positive culture in the workplace. This exemplifies the transforming potential of empathy, not only in the business sphere but also in other contexts.

Chapter 6:
Clarity

...

The story of Moses, a significant figure in the Bible, is spread across several chapters in the Old Testament, primarily in the books of Exodus, Leviticus, Numbers, and Deuteronomy. Moses played a crucial role in leading the Israelites out of slavery in Egypt and guiding them through the wilderness. While the entire narrative of Moses encompasses various aspects, including leadership, laws, and divine encounters, the theme of clarity can be observed in specific passages. Here are some key verses:

- Exodus 3:1-22: In this chapter, Moses encounters God in the burning bush. God communicates clearly with Moses, revealing His plan to deliver the Israelites and instructing Moses on his role.

- Exodus 4:1-17: Moses expresses concerns and uncertainties about his ability to communicate effectively. God provides clarity and assurance, even giving Moses signs to perform.

- Exodus 19:3-8: God communicates His covenant with the Israelites through Moses. The clarity of the covenant establishes the terms of their relationship with God.

- Exodus 34:27-35: Moses receives the Ten Commandments from God, representing a clear set of moral and ethical guidelines for the Israelites.

- Deuteronomy 6:1-9: Moses reiterates God's commands to the Israelites, emphasizing the importance of passing down clear instructions to future generations.

Moses' story is marked by moments of divine communication, where God provides clear guidance and instructions. These passages showcase the importance of clarity in leadership, communication, and the transmission of divine principles.

The story of Moses:

The narrative of Moses, which is included in the Bible, serves as a striking instance of the need for clarity in communication, particularly during periods of significant change and uncertainty.

Moses, who had been selected by God to lead the Israelites out of Egypt, was presented with the significant challenge of conveying the will of God to his people of Israel. It was through experiences such as the burning bush and the Ten Commandments that he was given heavenly direction. During their trip to the Promised Land, it was essential for him to be able to communicate these ideas in a way that was understandable to a varied and often obstinate group of followers.

In the context of the business world, the narrative of Moses demonstrates how important it is for leaders to employ communication strategies that are both clear and successful. The leaders of an organisation are obligated to effectively communicate their vision, goals, and expectations to their teams to successfully navigate organisational changes, transitions, or even day-to-day operations. When there is clarity in communication, there is less room for misunderstandings, errors are avoided, and unity and collaboration are fostered.

Moses's position as a communicator is demonstrated not only by his capacity to deliver messages from God but also by his leadership in mediating disagreements between the Israelites throughout their history. It was because of his ability to communicate clearly and solve problems that he was able to keep the community in a state of order and peace. This success highlights the significance of good communication in the process of conflict resolution.

A lesson that workers of corporations may learn from the narrative of Moses is that effective communication is an essential component of effective leadership. It enables leaders to explain their vision and expectations with clarity, so ensuring that their staff are well-informed and aligned with the objectives of the organisation. In addition, it highlights the need to maintain clarity in communication, which is not only essential during times of transition but also a continuing requirement for effective cooperation and healthy relationships in the business sector.

The narrative of Moses serves as a model for leaders and employees in the corporate environment, drawing their attention to the fact that good and clear communication is a fundamental component of success in any organisational setting. It indicates that the capacity to create a clear message may motivate, bring together, and direct a group of people towards the accomplishment of shared objectives by adhering to the rules that are provided below.

Clarity is the art of communicating in a way that is both clear and effective.

The lighthouse that guides communication across the tumultuous seas of misunderstanding and misinterpretation is clarity. This is especially important in the complex world of business settings.

This chapter examines the value of clarity in corporate communication, diving into the art of clear and successful communication and presenting solutions to overcome typical communication hurdles in the workplace. Specifically, the chapter focuses on the importance of effectively communicating with employees.

How to Communicate in a Way That Is Both Clear and Effective

The ability to communicate effectively is essential to the success of business environments. It gives individuals and teams the ability to work together, make decisions based on accurate information, and accomplish shared objectives. When it comes to ensuring that communications are correctly transmitted and received, clarity is the most important factor. We are going to learn how to communicate in a way that is both clear and successful.

- Accuracy: Accuracy in language and the delivery of messages is essential to communicating clearly. Messages must be clear and succinct, eliminating ambiguity and excessive jargon. It is possible to reduce the likelihood of misconceptions by communicating precisely.
- Characteristic of effective communicators is that they are aware of the context in which they are talking. They think about the people who will be receiving the message, the reason for the communication, and the medium that will be utilised to convey the information.
- Engaging in active listening: Effective communication is a process that goes in both directions. Active listening is an essential component since it guarantees that the person

receiving the message understands it and then allows them to provide comments or ask for clarification.

- Empathy: Empathy is an important component of good communication because it enables individuals to customise their communications to the cognitive and emotional requirements of the listener. Communication based on empathy helps to cultivate both understanding and trust.

Conquering Communication Obstacles Workplace Obstacles and Challenges

There is a possibility that impediments to communication will impede the flow of information in the workplace. The identification and resolution of these obstacles are necessary in order to preserve clarity and guarantee that messages are sent in a manner that is both accurate and efficient.

- **Language & Jargon:** Varying levels of linguistic proficiency and an excessive amount of jargon can sometimes make it difficult to communicate clearly. Among the solutions are the utilisation of language that is easy to comprehend, the provision of explanations for terminology that are peculiar to the sector, and the provision of language instruction when it is required.

- **Differences in Culture:** Misunderstandings might arise when there are a variety of cultures present in the workplace. Having open communication, being sensitive to cultural differences, and receiving cross-cultural training are all ways to help reduce these challenges.

- **An Overabundance of Information:** An excessive amount of information might result in one becoming confused and lacking clarity. Put material in order of importance and avoid overloading receivers with information that is not essential.
- **Distractions:** Distractions in the workplace, whether they are the real or digital variety, can make it difficult to communicate effectively. By reducing the number of distractions that occur during meetings and talks, you may encourage directed communication.

Obtaining Clarity: Obstacles to Overcome and Possible Solutions

- **Clarity**: is an essential component of business communication; nonetheless, it is not without its difficulties. Listed below are some of the most prevalent problems and possible solutions:
- **Erroneous interpretation:** Erroneous interpretation can arise when there are variations in how things are interpreted. To guarantee comprehension, some solutions include the utilisation of visual aids, the provision of examples, and the encouragement of active feedback.
- **Incomplete or ambiguous communications:** may be the result of a lack of feedback, which was mentioned in the previous point. In situations where receivers are unsure about a message, it is important to encourage them to seek clarification or request further information.

- **Emotional Barriers:** Emotional barriers have the potential to block straightforward communication, particularly when dealing with sensitive themes or circumstances that involve conflict. Through the cultivation of emotional intelligence and empathy, these obstacles can be overcome.
- **Resistance to Change:** One of the obstacles that might be encountered is resistance to changes in communication techniques. To facilitate transitions and encourage buy-in from members of the team, training and assistance should be provided.

When it comes to navigating the murky seas of business environments, clarity serves as the beacon that directs communication towards its destination. Accuracy, consciousness of the surrounding environment, attentive listening, and empathy are all required. In order to overcome communication hurdles, it is necessary to address linguistic and cultural differences, minimise information overload, and minimise distractions. Clear and effective communication is an invaluable tool for individuals and organisations that want to prosper in the business world. Despite the difficulties, the advantages of clear and effective communication make it an essential asset.

Clarity's ripple effect in corporate environments includes the following:

Within the context of business contexts, the consequences of clarity extend well beyond the interactions and communications of individual employees. There is a domino effect that occurs when there is clear communication in the workplace, which affects many different areas of the workplace, such as decision-making, problem-solving, and organisational culture.

- **Making Informed Decisions:** One of the benefits of clarity is that it guarantees decision-makers have access to information that is both accurate and pertinent. When decisions are made based on accurate information, the resulting plans and actions are more successful.
- **Effective problem-solving**: Is facilitated by clear communication, which is the second important factor. It is more probable that teams will be able to successfully collaborate to handle obstacles when they can comprehend the problems and approaches that have been suggested.
- **Responsibility:** Clarity is a factor that encourages responsibility. When individuals are provided with clear communication on their roles and expectations, they are more likely to take ownership of the work that they are assigned.
- **Culture of the Organisation:** A culture that encourages open and honest communication helps to cultivate trust, creativity, and transparency. The employees have the sense that they can express their thoughts and concerns, which contributes to a healthy culture inside the organisation.

Development of Clarity as a Skill That Lasts a Lifetime

Clarity is not only a one-time objective; rather, it is a talent that is present throughout one's whole life and calls for ongoing attention and growth.

- Active comments: In the context of communications, actively supporting comments and seeking clarity is encouraged. When someone is confused about something, they should feel that they may ask for extra information without feeling pressured.
- Training and Development: Organisations can offer training in effective communication, which may include methods for establishing clarity. These kinds of programmes can provide employees with the necessary abilities they require.
- Evaluations regularly: Evaluations of communication practices can assist people and organisations in determining areas in which clarity can be enhanced and in developing plans to address those areas.
- Documenting the Most Effective Methods: Creating a culture of continuous improvement within an organisation may be accomplished by documenting and sharing the best practices for clear communication within the organisation.

To summarise, the transformative power of clarity cannot be overstated.

When it comes to communication in business settings, clarity is the foundation of clear and successful communication. Accuracy, consciousness of the surrounding environment, attentive listening, and empathy are all required. To overcome communication hurdles, it is necessary to address linguistic and cultural differences, minimise information overload, and minimise distractions. The advantages of clear and effective communication make it an essential tool for individuals and organisations that are seeking success and progress in the business world. This is true even though it presents its own unique set of problems.

Clarity not only improves relationships between individuals and teams, but it also has an impact on decision-making, problem-solving, accountability, and the culture of an organisation. Because it is a skill that lasts a lifetime, clarity necessitates the provision of active feedback, training, consistent assessments, and the documenting of best practices to guarantee that it continues to serve as a guiding principle in the business environment. It is a monument to the transforming power of successful communication that clarity is a testament to. successful communication determines not just the success of businesses but also a harmonious and inventive culture in the workplace.

Chapter 7:
Self-Control

•••

The story of David and Goliath is found in the First Book of Samuel, specifically in 1 Samuel 17. This famous narrative illustrates courage, faith, and self-control in the face of adversity. While the theme of self-control might not be as explicit as in other stories, the underlying principles of David's character, restraint, and trust in God showcase elements of self-control.

- 1 Samuel 17:32-37: In these verses, David demonstrates self-control by confidently volunteering to face Goliath. Despite discouragement from King Saul, David maintains his composure and explains how God had delivered him from dangers in the past.
- 1 Samuel 17:45-47: As David faces Goliath, his words reflect a deep trust in God and a controlled determination to confront the giant. This moment reveals David's reliance on divine strength rather than his abilities.
- 1 Samuel 17:48-51: The actual confrontation with Goliath showcases David's skill with a sling, emphasizing precision and control over brute force.

While the story is often celebrated for David's bravery and trust in God, aspects of self-control can be observed in his calmness under pressure and his reliance on faith rather than fear. The narrative demonstrates that true strength lies not only in physical prowess but also in self-control and trust in a higher power.

The story of David and Goliath:

At the same time as it is a story of bravery, the story of David and Goliath is also a magnificent show of self-control in the face of overwhelming odds.

David, who was only a young shepherd at the time, was confronted by Goliath, a tough and veteran warrior who was of Philadelphian descent. David exhibited self-control by choosing an alternative method, which was in contrast to the normal approach, which would have been to engage in a direct fight. Instead of relying on his abilities and a straightforward sling and stones, he chose not to wear the cumbersome armour that was supplied to him.

When applied to the business world, the story of David and Goliath highlights the need to exercise self-control when it comes to making decisions and finding solutions to problems. In circumstances in which obstacles appear to be insurmountable, retaining composure and exercising self-control can enable one to come up with solutions that are more creative and efficient. It is illustrative of David's deliberate and controlled approach to problem-solving that he chose to utilise his talents and a stone that was well-aimed rather than participate in typical combat.

A further illustration of the need for self-control in leadership is provided by David's narrative. When he was a young shepherd, he seemed an odd choice to face a giant; yet, the combination of his self-control and his courage made him an extremely formidable contender for leadership. As a result, it demonstrates that self-control, when combined with drive and vision, has the potential to motivate others and result in extraordinary accomplishments.

The story of David and Goliath acts as a reminder to employees of corporations that self-control is necessary for logical decision-making, particularly in situations where there is a lot of pressure on them to make decisions. It teaches students to maintain their composure, evaluate the difficulties impartially, and think about other ways to approach the problem-solving process. The ability to exercise self-control is not limited to only repressing one's feelings; rather, it involves successfully channelling those feelings to accomplish one's objectives.

Employees of corporations are motivated to address issues with a level head and a strategic perspective as a result of David's narrative. It illustrates that self-control when paired with bravery and drive, may lead to success, even when confronted with challenges that appear to be insurmountable. This example demonstrates that self-control is an essential talent for both employees and leaders in the business sector to achieve success.

Self-control is a superpower that enables individuals to navigate the often tumultuous seas of stress, emotions, and professional obstacles in the ever-demanding corporate landscape. Self-control is a crucial factor in the success of individuals. The relevance of self-control in the management of emotions and the promotion of professional achievement is emphasised throughout this chapter, which delves into the crucial function that self-control plays in corporate settings.

Keeping Oneself Under Control in High-Stress Work Environments

The presence of stress is an ever-present companion in business environments; yet, the ability to exercise self-control is the guiding light that leads individuals through these turbulent seas. To better understand the role that self-control plays in stress management and prospering in demanding work circumstances, let's go deeper into this topic.

1. **Emotional Regulation:** Self-control gives people the ability to moderate their emotional reactions to the occurrence of stressful situations. As a result of their ability to behave deliberately and logically, they can reduce the emotional toll that stress has on them.

2. **Stress Resilience:** Stress resilience is influenced by one's ability to exercise self-control. People who can exercise self-control are better able to recover from stressful situations, therefore preserving their health and allowing them to concentrate on their work.

3. **The management of disputes:** In contexts of work that are very demanding, disagreements are unavoidable. Individuals can approach confrontations with composure and diplomacy when they have self-control, which ultimately leads to more productive settlements.

Self-control guarantees that individuals can make clear and sensible judgements even when they are under pressure, which enhances their professional performance. Stress can impair judgement, but self-control ensures that individuals can make decisions.

Controlling Your Feelings to Achieve Professional Success

Emotions are an inevitable component of the human experience, and the ability to successfully manage them is essential to achieving success in one's professional life. The ability to exercise self-control is the bridge that connects emotions to logic. It enables individuals to harness their emotions to produce positive results.

- **Emotional Intelligence:** One of the most important aspects of emotional intelligence is maintaining self-control. Individuals who possess a high level of emotional intelligence can identify, comprehend, and control their own emotions, as well as the emotions of others, which ultimately results in improved relationships with friends and family.
- **Communication:** When emotions are not properly regulated, effective communication is frequently negatively impacted. Individuals can improve their communication skills by exercising self-control, which enables them to communicate their views and ideas, even when confronted with emotionally charged circumstances.
- **Having self-control:** This is a great way to boost both your drive and your ability to concentrate. Even amid distractions or obstacles, individuals can maintain their dedication to the activities and objectives they have set for themselves.
- **Self-Control and Emotional Management:** Self-control and emotional management are both beneficial to personal growth. Individuals can gain knowledge from their emotional responses and utilise them as possibilities for advancement in their own lives.

Self-control: Obstacles to Overcome and Possible Solutions to Overcome Them

Although self-control is very necessary in business environments, it is not without its difficulties. Listed below are some of the most prevalent problems and possible solutions:

- **Overwhelming Stress:** An individual's capacity for self-control can be overwhelmed by excessive stress from a variety of sources. Techniques for managing stress, such as mindfulness and time management, as well as seeking help from supervisors or mentors, are among the solutions.
- **Emotional Triggers:** Certain circumstances or people have the potential to set off powerful emotional responses that make it difficult to exercise self-control. The solutions include identifying these triggers and creating techniques to control them, such as taking a step back or obtaining the perspective of someone from outside the situation.
- **Controlling negative emotions:** such as rage or impatience, may be especially difficult. Negative emotions include things like anger and frustration. Some of the strategies include developing self-awareness, learning tools for self-regulation, and, if necessary, obtaining professional counselling.
- **Inadequate Resources:** It is possible that certain persons may not have access to tools or support networks that can assist them in managing stress and exercising self-control. Training and tools may be made available by organisations to help employees in exercising self-control in the workplace.

The ability to exercise self-control is a crucial superpower that enables individuals to successfully navigate stress, exercise emotional control, and cultivate professional success in the business environment. It contributes to the control of emotions, the resistance to stress, the management of conflicts, and the ability to make successful decisions. The development of emotional intelligence, communication skills, motivation, and personal growth are all enhanced by self-control.

The cultivation of self-control requires the use of stress management strategies, the identification of emotional triggers, the management of negative emotions, and the utilisation of resources and support systems. Despite the difficulties, the benefits of self-control include professional success, well-being, effective communication, and personal development. As a result, self-control is an essential asset for both individuals and organisations operating in the business environment.

The Influence of Self-Control on the Environments of Corporations and Businesses

The importance of self-control in business settings extends well beyond the management of personal stress and the regulating of emotions shown by individuals. It creates a domino effect that affects many other areas of the workplace, such as leadership, teamwork, and the culture of the organisation.

- Self-controlled leaders can inspire their colleagues and lead by example, which is the first factor in leadership effectiveness. Their capacity to cope with feelings and maintain composure in the face of adversity contributes to the development of a culture that values reasonable and calm decision-making.
- Team Cohesion: Self-control is a factor that supports the cohesiveness of a team. When a leader can exercise self-control, there is a greater likelihood that members of the team will work together amicably and successfully settle issues.

- The settlement of conflicts: an essential component of successful conflict resolution is the exercise of self-control. Leaders who possess self-control can manage conflicts using the tactic of diplomacy and steer their teams towards beneficial solutions.
- Culture of the Organisation: A culture that encourages self-control is conducive to the development of emotional intelligence and personal growth. It helps to cultivate a workplace environment in which individuals can properly handle stress and emotions, which contributes to a positive culture inside the organisation.

How to Develop Self-Control as a Skill That Lasts a Lifetime

Self-control is not a fixed attribute but rather a talent that is acquired during one's whole life and requires ongoing development and progress.

1. Stress Management approaches: To improve their ability to exercise self-control in difficult work contexts, individuals can investigate various stress management approaches. Some examples of these techniques are mindfulness, time management, and physical activity.

2. Training in Emotional Intelligence: Individuals can acquire the abilities and tactics necessary to recognise, comprehend, and successfully control their emotions through participation in training programmes that focus on emotional intelligence.

3. A component of self-control is self-awareness: Which serves as the basis for self-control. People ought to make it a habit to review their emotional reactions regularly and look for possibilities to better themselves constantly.

4. Leadership Development: Leadership development programmes may help those who are already in positions of authority improve their ability to exercise self-control, which they can then go on to teach to their colleagues.

In a nutshell, the transformative power of self-control includes the following:

The superpower that enables individuals to handle stress, regulate emotions, and create professional achievement in the business environment is self-control. Self-control is the superpower that empowers individuals. Emotional control, stress resilience, conflict management, and effective decision-making are all improved as a result of this enhancement. The ability to exercise self-control is the bridge that connects emotions to logic. It enables individuals to harness their emotions to produce positive results.

The cultivation of self-control requires the use of skills for stress management, the identification of emotional triggers, the management of negative emotions, and the utilisation of resources and support networks through access. Despite the difficulties, the benefits of self-control include professional success, well-being, efficient communication, and personal development. As a result, self-control is a vital tool for individuals and organisations that want to prosper in the business world.

The influence of self-control extends beyond the benefits that it provides to individuals; it also has an impact on the efficacy of leadership, the cohesiveness of teams, the settlement of conflicts, and the culture of organisations. Because it is a talent that lasts a lifetime, self-control is something that has to be continually developed and grown to ensure that it continues to be a guiding principle in the business world. It is a demonstration of the transforming potential of self-control in business contexts as well as in places outside of them.

Chapter 8:

Building Lasting Relationships

• • •

The story of Paul and Timothy unfolds across various letters, particularly in the New Testament books of Acts, 1 Corinthians, Philippians, Colossians, 1 and 2 Timothy, and Philemon. While not a continuous narrative like some other biblical stories, the relationship between Paul, the apostle, and Timothy, his disciple and co-worker, is a central theme in several passages. Here are key verses that illuminate their relationship:

- Acts 16:1-3: This passage introduces Timothy as a disciple and notes Paul's decision to have him accompany the missionary journey, highlighting the beginning of their relationship.
- 1 Corinthians 4:14-17: In this section, Paul refers to Timothy as his beloved and faithful son in the Lord, emphasizing the depth of their spiritual relationship.
- Philippians 2:19-24: Paul expresses his intention to send Timothy to the Philippians, highlighting Timothy's genuine care for others and his proven character.
- 1 Timothy 1:2-3: In the opening of his letter to Timothy, Paul refers to him as his true child in the faith, emphasizing the spiritual aspect of their relationship.

- 2 Timothy 1:2-7: Paul's second letter to Timothy is filled with personal sentiments, expressing gratitude for Timothy's genuine faith and the spiritual inheritance passed down from his grandmother Lois and mother Eunice.
- Philemon 1:1-2: While this letter is primarily addressed to Philemon, Timothy is mentioned as a co-sender, emphasizing the communal aspect of their relationships in the context of the Christian community.

The relationship between Paul and Timothy serves as a model of mentorship, discipleship, and partnership in spreading the Christian message. These passages highlight the depth of their bond and the impact of their collaboration on building lasting relationships within the early Christian community.

The story of Paul and Timothy:

It is a monument to the power of mentoring, direction, and the establishment of long-lasting connections in the business world the relationship that existed between the Apostle Paul and his young protégé, Timothy, could be considered a model.

In the New Testament, Paul is shown as a more experienced and important Christian leader, but Timothy is portrayed as a younger follower. To facilitate Timothy's development as a leader, Paul took Timothy under his wing, mentored him, and gave him advice. The upshot of this alliance was a tight and long-lasting connection that was founded on trust and principles that were held in common.

In the context of the business world, the narrative of Paul and Timothy might be interpreted as a model for mentorship and the cultivation of relationships inside organisations. In addition to fostering a feeling of continuity and knowledge transfer inside the organisation, providing younger employees with an effective mentoring programme may contribute to the professional and personal growth of those individuals.

Additionally, the guidance that Paul provided to Timothy and the friendship that he shared with Timothy shed insight into the value of establishing long-lasting partnerships. When it comes to the business sector, cultivating strong and long-lasting connections with coworkers, clients, and mentors may result in chances for personal development, professional progress, and professional growth.

The narrative of Paul and Timothy serves as a teaching tool for employees of corporations, encouraging them to seek out chances for mentoring and to be open to receiving instruction from colleagues who have more experience. The significance of making an investment in relationships and maintaining those ties over time is brought into focus by this.

By analysing the dynamics of the connection between Paul and Timothy, workers of corporations may get an understanding of how mentoring and the cultivation of long-lasting relationships help the development of both personal and professional skills. These connections have the potential to serve as a support system that not only helps individuals advance their careers but also helps to cultivate a feeling of unity and continuity inside an organisation.

This chapter emphasizes the significance of establishing relationships that are both long-lasting and significant in the business world. Employees are encouraged to seek out mentors, to be receptive to advice, and to engage in creating relationships inside their organisations, all of which have the potential to have a significant influence on their careers and the success of their organisations. All of this is attainable by adhering to the criteria that are listed below:

The power of effective communication in the workplace is a key factor in the development of long-lasting relationships.

The establishment of long-term connections is an endeavour that is of great value in the business world and extends beyond the realm of transactions and negotiations. The purpose of this chapter is to investigate the profound impact that good communication has on the development of supportive and harmonious corporate environments, as well as the strengthening of relationships within the workplace.

How Relationships in the Workplace Can Be Strengthened Through Effective Communication

Interpersonal connections in the workplace are the bedrock upon which a prosperous and pleasant business environment is built. The ability to communicate effectively is the glue that holds these connections together, which in turn makes them longer-lasting and more productive.

1. **Trust and Credibility:** Effective communication helps to develop trust and credibility among coworkers, bosses, and members of the team. The cultivation of trust occurs when persons interact in a manner that is honest, open, and consistent.

2. **Conflict Resolution:** Conflicts are an unavoidable component of the dynamics experienced in the workplace. The ability to communicate effectively equips individuals with the tools

necessary to confront and resolve disputes through diplomatic means, therefore preserving and even enhancing relationships.

3. Collaboration and Teamwork: The ability to communicate effectively is necessary for successful collaboration and teamwork. Cooperation thrives when members of a team openly interact with one another, exchange knowledge with one another, and actively listen to one another.

4. Understanding and Empathy: Compassion, which is an essential component of successful communication, is the road that leads to a deeper comprehension. People can cultivate stronger connections with one another when they demonstrate active listening, take into consideration the opinions of others, and speak with empathy.

The establishment of a business environment that is both supportive and harmonious

Strong connections, good communication, and a culture of respect are the defining characteristics of a business environment that is supportive and harmonious towards its employees. It is a fertile field for the development of inventions, partnerships, and achievements.

- **Open discourse:** A culture that promotes open discourse allows individuals to freely share their opinions, ideas, and concerns without the fear of being punished financially or otherwise. As a result, the working environment becomes more welcoming and pleasant after this.
- **Inclusivity:** An atmosphere that is harmonious places a high emphasis on variety and prioritises inclusiveness. It

is possible to cultivate a culture of support when all voices are included in the conversation and when people from different backgrounds are treated with respect.

- **Constructive feedback**: This is an essential component of an atmosphere that is helpful, and it provides an opportunity for growth. Individuals are encouraged to acquire and enhance the skills they already possess, which results in chances for both personal and professional development.
- **Conflict as an Opportunity for progress:** A supportive business environment views disagreements not as something that causes disruptions but rather as chances for progress. Constructively, conflicts are managed, which ultimately results in improved understanding and stronger relationships.

Developing Long-Lasting Relationships: Obstacles to Overcome and Possible Solutions

The establishment of long-lasting connections in the workplace can be fraught with difficulties; nevertheless, these difficulties can be overcome through the application of efficient tactics.

- **Obstacles to Communication:** Language hurdles, variations in communication styles, and technical obstacles are all factors that might impede successful communication. Several potential solutions include language instruction, communication workshops, and the use of communication technologies that are simple to use.
- **Resistance to Change:** Employees or leaders may be resistant to the implementation of changes that are

intended to improve communication and relationships. Through communication and training, the shift may be made easier, and buy-in from all parties involved can be encouraged.

- **Misunderstandings:** Misunderstandings have the potential to cause relationships to become strained. To reduce the number of misconceptions that occur, encourage folks to seek clarification, ask questions, and offer feedback.
- **Bias and Inequality:** Both biases and inequalities have the potential to damage romantic relationships. Training on diversity and inclusion should be encouraged, inequities should be monitored, and policies that address prejudices should be implemented to promote a fairer working environment.

The establishment of long-lasting connections in the business sector is a worthwhile endeavour that may be made feasible via the utilisation of efficient communication. Building trust, resolving disagreements, encouraging cooperation, and cultivating empathy are all outcomes that may be achieved via effective communication. Furthermore, it contributes to the establishment of a supportive and harmonious corporate atmosphere that is characterised by open communication, inclusion, feedback, and progress. For cultivating long-lasting and fruitful relationships in the workplace, it is possible to overcome challenges such as obstacles to communication, reluctance to change, misconceptions, and inequity via the application of intelligent tactics.

The Effects That Will Be Caused When Effective Communication Is Used in the Workplace

When it comes to the workplace, the importance of excellent communication extends well beyond the exchanges that occur between individuals. Leadership, teamwork, and the entire culture of the company are all impacted as a result of its ripple effect across the organisation.

- **A transition in leadership is frequently the result of effective communication**: Which in turn leads to increased leadership. When leaders demonstrate the ability to actively listen, communicate in a way that is both clear and empathic, and constructively resolve issues, they inspire trust and loyalty among their people.
- **Team Synergy:** Effective communication is a key factor in the development of team synergy. By communicating honestly with one another, sharing their expertise, and listening to one another, members of a team can work more effectively, which ultimately leads to enhanced team dynamics and performance.
- **The ability to communicate effectively enables informed and inclusive decision-making**: Which is the third benefit of effective communication. Organisations are better able to make decisions that are well-rounded and productive when they foster different viewpoints and make sure that all voices are heard.
- **Positive Corporate Culture:** A culture of a company that is characterised by excellent communication is more likely to be considered positive and harmonious. It places high importance on open communication, inclusiveness,

and feedback, all of which contribute to the growth and happiness of its workforce.

The Development of Effective Communication as a Skill That Lasts a Lifetime

The ability to communicate effectively is a talent that may be developed over one's whole life and requires continuous devotion and improvement.

1. **Engaging in active listening:** One of the most important aspects of successful communication is active listening. Individuals need to make a concerted effort to improve their listening skills by practising techniques such as remaining present throughout talks and making an effort to comprehend before answering.

2. **Instruction in Conflict Resolution:** The ability to resolve conflicts is an essential component of successfully communicating with others. Individuals can be assisted in addressing differences constructively by receiving training in approaches to conflict resolution.

3. **Leadership Development:** Programmes that are designed to train leaders typically contain elements that are connected to effective communication capabilities. Leaders can improve their communication skills by participating in these programmes, which may then be shared with their staff.

4. **Inclusion and Diversity Promotion**: Training is necessary because good communication is necessary for promoting diversity and inclusion. The training that is provided in this area may assist individuals in recognising their prejudices, communicating more inclusively, and creating more equal settings.

In Conclusion: The Power of Establishing Relationships That Will Last a Lifetime

The establishment of long-lasting connections within the context of the business world is not only a personal objective; rather, it is an indispensable basis for the development of a mutually supportive and harmonious corporate culture. When it comes to this endeavour, effective communication plays a key role, as it helps to develop trust, resolve problems, enhance teamwork, and cultivate empathy.

Using tactics that are well thought out, it is possible to effectively address challenges that arise in the process of establishing long-lasting relationships. These challenges include obstacles to communication, reluctance to change, misconceptions, and inequalities. The ripple effect of successful communication extends to the transformation of leadership, the synergy of teams, the enhancement of decision-making, and the creation of a good corporate culture. This makes it possible to create a working environment in which connections are fostered and professional development and achievement are acknowledged. A monument to the transforming potential of excellent communication in the business world and beyond, it serves as an example of how successful communication can be.

End of Note:

...

We are grateful for your company as we conclude "**The Biblical Blueprint for Corporate Success**" - ***Timeless Wisdom for Effective Communication***. We hope the wisdom from aged values resonates with you and demonstrates the way biblical teachings apply to modern business.

When we consider the strength of these timeless principles, we are reminded of "**Leadership Lessons from the Bible**" - ***Insights for Becoming an Effective Leader***. This predecessor to our current endeavour explored leadership's essence by providing aged wisdom. Leadership lessons from the previous journey have grown in this new exploration.

As you conclude "**The Biblical Blueprint for Corporate Success,**" evaluate how biblical lessons might change your work life. This message transcends belief and culture, promoting universal guidelines for interpersonal interaction, collaboration, and leadership.

We wrote these pages to give you professional knowledge and abilities. We encourage you to implement "Leadership Lessons from the Bible." Both books integrate to offer a comprehensive guide to ethical communication, compassionate relationships, and effective leadership.

We recommend carrying these lessons as you manage the complexity of business. Applying biblical principles to communication and relationships leads to personal and professional success and helps create an ethical and harmonious business culture.

Our best wishes for your business success and fulfilment. Let these eternal ideas guide your ongoing experience. May the wisdom of the centuries guide you to long-term success and lasting professional connections.

With sincere regards,

Pradeep Kasab

Author, "Leadership Lessons from the Bible"